SCHOLASTIC

M000250916

2

Great Grammar Practice

Linda Ward Beech

New York • Toronto • London • Auckland • Sydney
New Delhi • Mexico City • Hong Kong • Buenos Aires

Teaching
Resources

Edited by Mela Ottaiano
Cover design by Michelle Kim
Interior design by Melinda Belter

ISBN: 978-0-545-79422-0
Copyright © 2015 by Scholastic Inc.
Illustrations copyright © by Scholastic Inc.
All rights reserved.
Published by Scholastic Inc.
Printed in the U.S.A.

3 4 5 6 7 8 9 10   40   22 21 20 19 18 17

Contents

Introduction

To be successful at any task, it is important to have the right tools and skills. Grammar is one of the basic tools of written and oral language. Students need to learn and practice key grammar skills to communicate effectively. The pages in this book provide opportunities to introduce and/or expand students' familiarity with grammar rules and concepts.

Using This Book

If your class has grammar texts, you can duplicate the pages in this book to use as reinforcements.

✏️ Read aloud the instructions and examples as much of the material will be new to second graders. If necessary, provide additional examples and answer students' questions.

✏️ Model how to do the activity.

You can add these pages as assignments to your writing program and keep copies in skills folders at your writing resource center.

You may also want to use the activities as a class lesson or have students complete the pages in small groups.

Page by Page

You can use these suggestions to help students complete the activity pages.

Activity 1
Review the examples to help students understand why one group of words makes a sentence and the other does not.

Activity 2
Emphasize that word order in a sentence makes a difference in meaning.

Activity 3
Point out that the subject is one of the main parts of a sentence.

Activity 4
Tell students that the parts they are adding to the sentences are called predicates. A predicate contains the action in a sentence.

Activity 5
Students may need assistance in forming the sentences. Point out that they should choose the best answer, even if more than one makes sense.

Activity 6
Remind students that there are different kinds of sentences. Statements and questions are the most common kinds.

Activity 7
Point out that capitalization and punctuation help readers know when a sentence begins and ends.

Activity 8
Ask students to think of other examples of commands and exclamations.

Activity 9
Point out that if it is said with feeling, a command can also end with an exclamation mark.

Activities 10 and 11

Mention that the sentences on these pages are called compound sentences; each of the two ideas has a subject and a predicate. Invite students to read aloud the sentences they write for Part B.

Activity 12

Review the characteristics of statements, questions, commands, and exclamations. Remind students that each type of sentence has its own special punctuation.

Activity 13

Encourage students to find examples of nouns in their reading books.

Activity 14

Explain that most nouns are common nouns; proper nouns are specific names for a given person, place, or thing.

Activity 15

Tell students that a noun that names one thing is singular; a noun that names more than one thing is plural.

Activity 16

Mention that the noun plurals on this page are called irregular plurals because they are not formed like regular plural nouns. It is important to memorize these plurals.

Activity 17

Tell students there are many other names for groups of animals. Students might enjoy finding and illustrating additional examples.

Activity 18

Stress that possessive nouns are different than plural nouns.

Activity 19

Point out that the pronouns *he*, *she*, and *it* are singular, while the pronoun *they* is plural.

Activity 20

Point out that the pronouns *I* and *me* are singular. The pronoun *we* is plural, and the pronoun *you* can be singular or plural.

Activity 21

Reflexive pronouns are often confusing. Watch for incorrect usage when students are speaking.

Activity 22

Review the purpose of a noun and a pronoun. Remind students that the pronoun must agree with the noun it replaces.

Activity 23

Review with students that a verb shows action. Point out that the verbs in this activity show action that happened in the past.

Activity 24

Some students have difficulty with noun-verb agreement. You might do this exercise aloud with the class so students can hear the correct agreement and talk about why a verb is singular or plural in each sentence.

Activity 25

Introduce the term *verb tense* when presenting this page. Explain that it refers to time, or when the action takes place.

Activity 26

Invite students to read aloud the sentences they write for Part B.

Activity 27

Mention that the past verb forms on this page are called irregular verbs because the past tenses are not formed like regular verbs. It is important to memorize these irregular verbs.

Activity 28

The verbs on this page are forms of the verb *to be* and are often used incorrectly. You might do this exercise aloud with the class so students can hear the correct agreement and talk about why a verb is singular or plural in each sentence.

Great Grammar Practice, Grade 2 © 2015 by Scholastic Teaching Resources

Activity 29

The verbs on this page are often used incorrectly. You might do this exercise aloud with the class so students can hear the correct agreement and talk about why a verb is singular or plural in each sentence.

Activities 30 and 31

Mention that the word *not* means "no." Point out that the pronunciations of *don't* and *won't* are different from the way other contractions are pronounced.

Activity 32

Let students know that two of the verbs in the word bank will not be used. Invite students to identify the contractions in the word bank.

Activity 33

Explain that adjectives add detail to nouns by telling more about them.

Activity 34

Invite students to use the back of their paper and crayons or colored pencils to illustrate the sentences in Part B.

Activity 35

Check that students choose appropriate adjectives for the pictures in Part B.

Activities 36 and 37

Suggest that students ask themselves "When? Where? How?" when trying to identify adverbs.

Activity 38

Invite students to think of other adverbs they might use with the verbs in Part B.

Activity 39

Review what a noun and a verb are before introducing this page.

Activities 40–42

Explain that prepositions and the phrases they introduce help make a sentence more interesting and informative.

Activity 43

Review the different times to use capitals: at the beginnings of sentences, with proper nouns, and for the pronoun *I*.

Activity 44

Remind students that a comma is a form of punctuation. Review the punctuation that students know: period, question mark, exclamation mark, and apostrophe. Point out that a comma occurs in the middle of a sentence, not at the end like a period.

Activity 45

Point out the different parts of a date—the month, day, and year—and the order in which students should write them. As a class, practice writing a few dates before students complete this page.

Activity 46

Before students complete this page, review that proper nouns begin with capital letters, and a sentence begins with a capital letter.

Activity 47

Review the different ways to use an apostrophe: to form a possessive noun or a contraction.

Activity 48

Ask students to share what they know about the characteristics of statements, questions, commands, and exclamations. Be sure they can identify the punctuation that goes with each type of sentence.

Activity 49

Encourage students to find and write other words spelled with these vowel sounds.

Activity 50

Encourage students to find and write other words spelled with these blended sounds.

Activity 51

Invite students to go on a word hunt to find other words with double letters.

Great Grammar Practice, Grade 2 © 2015 by Scholastic Teaching Resources

Activity 52

Ask students to write a sentence using one of the nouns or plural nouns they made. Invite them to share their sentence with the class.

Activities 53 and 54

Point out the words in the word bank. Have students identify the base words.

Activity 55

Part B of this page offers students an opportunity to use dictionaries and to expand their vocabulary. Review how the words in a dictionary are organized and ask students to find more words beginning with these blends.

Connections to the Standards

With the goal of providing students nationwide with a quality education that prepares them for college and careers, broad standards were developed to establish rigorous educational expectations. These standards serve as the basis of many state standards. The chart below details how the activities in this book align with specific language and foundational skills standards for students in grade 2.

	English Language Arts Standards	Activities
Language	**Conventions of Standard English**	
	• Demonstrate command of the conventions of standard English grammar and usage when writing or speaking.	1–55
	• Demonstrate command of the conventions of standard English capitalization, punctuation, and spelling when writing.	7, 9, 12, 14, 18, 30, 31, 43–55
	Knowledge of Language	
	• Use knowledge of language and its conventions when writing, speaking, reading, or listening.	1–55
	Vocabulary Acquisition and Use	
	• Determine or clarify the meaning of unknown and multiple-meaning words and phrases based on grade 2 reading and content, choosing flexibly from an array of strategies.	3, 4, 13, 14, 17, 21, 23, 25, 32, 33, 35–42, 47, 49, 51–55
	• Demonstrate understanding of word relationships and nuances in word meanings.	1–55
	• Use words and phrases acquired through conversations, reading and being read to, and responding to texts, including using adjectives and adverbs to describe.	1–55
Foundational Skills	**Phonics and Word Recognition**	
	• Know and apply grade-level phonics and word analysis skills in decoding words.	16, 27, 31, 49–55
	Fluency	
	• Read with sufficient accuracy and fluency to support comprehension.	1–55

Great Grammar Practice, Grade 2 © 2015 by Scholastic Teaching Resources

Name _____ Date _____

What Is a Sentence?

A sentence is a group of words that tells a complete idea.

Sentence: The fireworks are loud.

Not a Sentence: The fireworks.

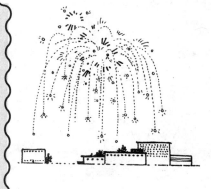

A. Write **sentence** or **not a sentence**.

1. The colors are bright. _____

2. Fireworks streak through the dark. _____

3. Fireworks light up the night. _____

4. Fall to the ground. _____

5. High in the sky. _____

6. People watch in delight. _____

B. Add words to make sentences.

7. The noise _____ .

8. _____ are red, yellow, and green.

Name _____ Date _____

In Order

> The order of words tells what a sentence means.
>
> **Sentence:** Maisie has a camera.
>
> **Not a Sentence:** Camera Maisie has a.

Underline under the words that make a sentence.

1. **a.** Maisie takes good pictures.

   b. Good Maisie pictures takes.

2. **a.** Subject she a chooses.

   b. She chooses a subject.

3. **a.** She looks through the lens.

   b. Through she looks the lens.

4. **a.** The shot right to get it is hard.

   b. It is hard to get the right shot.

5. **a.** The shutter she snaps.

   b. She snaps the shutter.

6. **a.** A picture appears.

   b. Appears a picture.

Name _____ Date _____

Sentence Subjects

The subject of a sentence tells who or what does something.

The dog watches the cat.

↑
subject of sentence

Add a subject to each sentence.
Use the picture to help you.

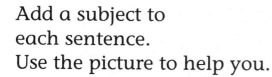

1. A _____ looks at his glasses.

2. The _____ has a teddy bear.

3. One _____ opens his suitcase.

4. _____ holds his skateboard.

5. A _____ wants food in her dish.

6. Her _____ is empty.

7. The _____ will wear her hat.

8. The _____ holds a bone.

Great Grammar Practice, Grade 2 © 2015 by Scholastic Teaching Resources

Name _____ Date _____

Sentence Action

Some words in a sentence tell what happens.

A faucet drips.

↑ what happens

WORD BANK

bounces	rocks
waves	sweeps
rings	ticks
cools	measures

Tell what happens in each sentence. Use the word bank.

 **1.** A fan _____ .

 **2.** A broom _____ .

 3. A ball _____ .

 4. A bell _____ .

 5. A flag _____ .

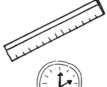 **6.** A ruler _____ .

 7. A clock _____ .

 8. A cradle _____ .

Great Grammar Practice, Grade 2 © 2015 by Scholastic Teaching Resources

Name _____ Date _____

Sentence Parts

A sentence has two parts.

One part is the subject.

The other part tells what the subject does.

The hikers saw an empty cabin.

subject · what happens

Draw a line to match the two parts of each sentence.

1. A loose shutter

2. The air

3. A mouse

4. Weeds

5. Dust

6. Old curtains

7. The floorboards

8. A cobweb

a. grew over the path.

b. covered the furniture.

c. ran into a hole.

d. banged.

e. sagged at the windows.

f. smelled musty.

g. was on the ceiling.

h. creaked loudly.

Great Grammar Practice, Grade 2 © 2015 by Scholastic Teaching Resources

Name _____ Date _____

Statements and Questions

A sentence that tells something is a **statement**.

A sentence that asks something is a **question**.

Statement: The water was chilly.

Question: Was the water chilly?

A. Read each sentence. Write **statement** or **question**.

1. Max jumped into the pool. _____

2. It was a cool day. _____

3. How did the water feel? _____

4. How long did Max stay in the pool? _____

5. He swam for a long time. _____

6. Did he get sick? _____

B. Complete the statement and question.

7. Max needed _____ .

8. Will he _____?

Name _____ Date _____

Writing Statements and Questions

A sentence always begins with a capital letter.

A statement ends with a period.

A question ends with a question mark.

Statement: It's time for the race.

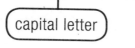
capital letter

period

Question: Will the runners line up?

capital letter

question mark

Write the sentences so that they begin and end correctly.

1. how many runners are on a team

_____

2. how far will they run

_____

3. the race is on the track

_____

4. is everyone ready

_____

Great Grammar Practice, Grade 2 © 2015 by Scholastic Teaching Resources

Name _____   Date _____

More Kinds of Sentences

A command is a sentence that tells what to do.

The subject of a command is *you*, but it is not said or written.

Command: Set the table.

The subject *you* is not stated.

An exclamation is a sentence that shows strong feeling.

Exclamation: That's great!

A. Read each sentence. Write **statement** or **command**.

1. Don't forget the napkins.   _____

2. Use the blue plates.   _____

3. The forks go on the left.   _____

4. The table looks nice.   _____

B. Read each sentence. Write **command** or **exclamation**.

5. Wow!   _____

6. Put glasses on the table.   _____

7. Please sit down.   _____

8. Thanks!   _____

    Great Grammar Practice, Grade 2 © 2015 by Scholastic Teaching Resources

Name _____   Date _____

Writing Commands and Exclamations

A sentence always begins with a capital letter.

A command ends with a period.

An exclamation ends with an exclamation mark.

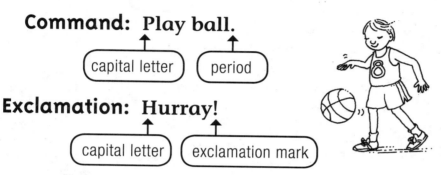

Command: Play ball.

capital letter   period

Exclamation: Hurray!

capital letter   exclamation mark

Write the sentences so that they begin and end correctly.

1. pass the ball _____

2. wow _____

3. guard that player _____

4. nice play _____

5. make that shot _____

6. great game _____

Name _____ Date _____

Sentences With *And*

The word *and* can link ideas in a sentence.

Mrs. Hill went to a store, and she bought beets.

      (idea 1)   (linking word)   (idea 2)

A. Add **and** to link the two ideas in each sentence. Then number the two ideas.

  1. The beets were red, _____ they were ripe.

      idea ____   idea ____

  2. Mrs. Hill paid for the beets, _____ she took them home.

      idea ____   idea ____

  3. She put the beets in a pot, _____ they were soon boiling.

      idea ____   idea ____

  4. The beets colored the water, _____ Mrs. Hill had a pink dye.

      idea ____   idea ____

B. Add an idea to complete each sentence.

  5. Mrs. Hill got some cloth, and _____.

  6. The cloth was pretty, and _____.

Sentences With *Because*

The word *because* can link ideas in a sentence.

Walt put on earmuffs because it was cold.

idea 1   linking word   idea 2

A. Add **because** to link the two ideas in each sentence.
Number the two ideas in each sentence.

1. Walt wore boots _____ the snow was wet.
     idea ____   idea ____

2. His scarf got damp _____ it dragged in the snow.
     idea ____   idea ____

3. His hands were cold _____ he forgot his mittens.
     idea ____   idea ____

4. Walt's head was warm _____ he wore a hat.
     idea ____   idea ____

B. Add an idea to complete each sentence.

5. Walt took a walk because _____.

6. His mother called him because _____.

Name _____   Date _____

Review: Sentences

> A sentence that tells something is a statement.
>
> A sentence that asks something is a question.
>
> A command is a sentence that tells what to do.
>
> The subject of a command is *you,* but it is not said or written.
>
> An exclamation is a sentence that shows strong feeling.

A. Read each sentence. Write **statement**, **question**, **command**, or **exclamation**. Add the correct end punctuation mark.

1. We're going to the playground___   _____

2. When are we going___   _____

3. Put your shoes on___   _____

4. Did you see the slide___   _____

5. Wow___   _____

6. It is very tall___   _____

B. Write the words and punctuation mark in order so that they form a sentence.

7. ate . our We at park lunch the

_____

Great Grammar Practice, Grade 2 © 2015 by Scholastic Teaching Resources

Name _____   Date _____

What Is a Noun?

A noun is a word that names
a person, place, or thing.

Person: girl
Place: school
Thing: pencil

A. Look at the picture above. Circle the noun
that answers each question.

1. Who is in the picture?   doctor   policeman   riding

2. What place is shown?   farm   strong   city

3. What thing is in the picture?   saddle   later   help

B. Write a noun from the word bank to complete each sentence.

4. The _____ walks along.

5. His _____ waves back and forth.

6. The _____ is empty.

7. A man looks out his _____.

8. A _____ floats by a building.

WORD BANK	
blue	bicycle
horse	window
street	tail
cloud	sunny

Great Grammar Practice, Grade 2 © 2015 by Scholastic Teaching Resources

Name _____ Date _____

Proper Nouns

> A proper noun is the specific name for a person, place or thing.
>
> A proper noun can also be the name of a place or a holiday.
>
> Each word in a proper noun begins with a capital letter.
>
> **Proper Nouns: Jeff Young, Mona Lang, Seattle, Halloween**

A. Circle the proper nouns in each sentence.

1. Becca Hardy went to the Rocky Mountains with her family.

2. They also visited Salt Lake City and San Francisco.

3. Mia Grasso joined them for Columbus Day.

B. Write the name of a holiday for each clue.

 4. Eat turkey. _____

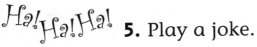 **5.** Play a joke. _____

 6. Watch fireworks. _____

 7. Make a heart. _____

C. Write the name of your city.

8. _____

Great Grammar Practice, Grade 2 © 2015 by Scholastic Teaching Resources

Name _____ Date _____

Plural Nouns

A plural noun names more than one person, place, or thing.

Most plural nouns end in -s.

One: pretzel

More Than One: pretzels

A. Circle the plural noun or nouns in each sentence.

1. Nick brought nuts for his snack. **2.** Ezra had bags of beans.

3. Where are Amy's carrots? **4.** We bought hotdogs and rolls.

B. Write the correct noun form in each sentence.

5. Dad ate a bunch of _____ .

grape   grapes

6. We had a good _____ at lunch.

cheese   cheeses

7. Mom made two _____ for the fair.

cake   cakes

8. How many _____ did you sell?

pie   pies

Name _____ Date _____

More Plural Nouns

Some nouns have different plural forms.

SINGULAR	PLURAL
child	children
woman	women
man	men
mouse	mice

SINGULAR	PLURAL
foot	feet
ox	oxen
tooth	teeth
goose	geese

Write each sentence so that the underlined nouns are plural.

1. The goose flew over the house.

_____

2. The child chased after the ball.

_____

3. The mouse ran when the woman screamed.

_____

4. The man hitched the ox to a cart.

_____

5. The sock covered Ella's foot.

_____

Great Grammar Practice, Grade 2 © 2015 by Scholastic Teaching Resources

Name _____ Date _____

Names for Groups

Some nouns name groups of animals.

ANIMAL	GROUP NAME
fish	school
lion	pride
bee	swarm
dog	pack

ANIMAL	GROUP NAME
sheep	flock
ant	army
ape	troop
goose	gaggle

A. Write a group noun for each animal.

1. A group of sheep is called a _____.

2. Lions live together in a _____.

3. A _____ of fish is a group of them.

4. A group of geese swimming is a _____.

B. Write the plural noun for an animal in each sentence.

5. An army of _____ came to our picnic.

6. We saw a troop of _____ in a movie.

7. A swarm of _____ flew to the hive.

8. A pack of _____ ran in the street.

Possessive Nouns

A possessive noun shows who owns something.
The noun ends with an apostrophe and an *s*: **'s**.

the boy's bike   **The bike belongs to the boy.**

↑

apostrophe and *s* show possession

A. Circle the word in each sentence that shows who owns something.

1. Jamie's bike is red.

2. His brother's bike has three wheels.

3. His friend's bike is gray.

4. Dad's bike needs a repair.

B. Read the first sentence. Then add a possessive noun to the second sentence.

5. The bell belonging to Mom is shiny.

   It is _____ bell.

6. That helmet belongs to Ada.

   It is _____ helmet.

Name _____ Date _____

What Is a Pronoun?

> A pronoun takes the place of a noun or nouns.
>
> *He, she, they,* and *it* are pronouns.
>
> **Carson went to the park. He went on the slide.**
>
> ↑ noun
>
> ↑ pronoun takes place of noun

A. Underline the noun in the first sentence. Circle the pronoun that replaces that noun in the second sentence.

1. The swing was empty. Carson hopped on it.

2. Carson swung high. He could see far away.

3. Some kids came by. They rode around on scooters.

4. Polly showed up. She was happy to see Carson.

B. Read the first sentence. Then complete the second sentence with **He, She, They,** or **It**.

5. Carson was hungry. _____ took out some pretzels.

6. Polly smiled. _____ wanted some too.

7. The sun disappeared. _____ went behind a cloud.

8. Polly and Carson left. _____ went home together.

Name _____ Date _____

More Pronouns

> A pronoun takes the place of a noun or nouns.
>
> *I, me, you,* and *we* are pronouns.
>
> **"I will measure you," Jada told Owen.**
>
> [pronoun replaces Jada's name]   [pronoun replaces Owen's name]

Circle the pronoun in each sentence. Write the name of the person or persons the pronoun replaces.

1. Jada said, "I am growing." _____

2. "Yes, you are," agreed Owen. _____

3. "How tall are you?" asked Jada. _____

4. "Measure me," said Owen. _____

5. "Okay, I will," Jada said. _____

6. "Please stand next to me," Jada added. _____

7. "We can take turns," Owen suggested. _____

8. "You are very tall," Jada said. _____

Great Grammar Practice, Grade 2 © 2015 by Scholastic Teaching Resources

Name _____ Date _____

Pronouns With Endings

Some pronouns end with *self*.

These pronouns tell more about the sentence subject.

I can mop the floor by myself.

subject   pronoun tells more about subject

Write a pronoun from the word bank to complete each sentence.

1. Fran raked the leaves by _____ .

2. Can Josh carry the tray by _____ ?

3. Neil and Roger pulled the wagons _____ .

4. The ball rolled by _____ down the hill.

5. I put the umbrella up by _____ .

6. Did you wash the dog by _____ ?

7. We did it by _____ .

Review: Nouns and Pronouns

A noun is a word that names a person, place, or thing.

A pronoun takes the place of the name of a person, place, or thing.

Read each pair of sentences. Circle the pronoun in the second sentence of each pair. Then write what noun the pronoun stands for.

1. Wyatt did not like to clean his room.

He liked a messy room.   _____

2. Mother wanted Wyatt to do some work.

She handed Wyatt a broom.   _____

3. The pigs came into Wyatt's room.

They helped Wyatt clean the room.   _____

4. Then Wyatt and the pigs played a game.

Wyatt and the pigs had fun playing it.   _____

5. The pigs and Wyatt played for a long time.

They liked to play games.   _____

6. Wyatt was sad to see his friends go.

He liked playing with the pigs.   _____

Great Grammar Practice, Grade 2 © 2015 by Scholastic Teaching Resources

Name _____ Date _____

What Is a Verb?

> A verb is a word that tells what someone or something does.
>
> Every sentence has a verb.
>
> **Marco cut a flower for his teacher.**
>
> ⌐verb⌐

A. Circle the verb in each sentence.

1. The flower needed water.

2. It drooped in Marco's hand.

3. Kiri gave Marco a wet paper towel.

4. The flower got water from the towel.

5. Marco took the flower to school safely.

WORD BANK

thanked	won
helped	put
liked	fed

B. Write a verb from the word bank to complete each sentence.

6. Mrs. Hill _____ the flower.

7. The teacher _____ the flower in a vase.

8. She _____ Marco for the gift.

   Great Grammar Practice, Grade 2 © 2015 by Scholastic Teaching Resources

Noun and Verb Agreement

> A verb showing the action of one person or thing ends in *-s*.
>
> A verb showing the action of more than one person or thing does not end in *-s*.
>
> **The wolf looks happy. The pigs talk to the wolf.**
>
> (shows action of one)   (shows action of more than one)

Write the correct verb form in each sentence.

1. The three pigs _____ Wally Wolf.

                         fear   fears

2. He _____ to eat pigs.

              like   likes

3. Parker Pig _____ a straw house.

                   build   builds

4. Penny Pig _____ a wood house.

                 make   makes

5. The wolf _____ their houses.

             destroy   destroys

6. Can the pigs _____ Wally?

                 fool   fools

7. Peter Pig _____ a stone house for

              design   designs

all of them.

Name _____ Date _____

Past and Present Tense Verbs

Verbs can tell about action in the present and the past.

Most past tense verbs end in *-ed*.

Present: walk   walks

Past: walked

A. Circle the verb in each sentence. Write **present** or **past** to tell about the verb tense.

1. Fiona waits at the stoplight. _____

2. A police officer directs traffic. _____

3. Many people fill the busy sidewalk. _____

4. Once, Fiona arrived late for her music lesson. _____

5. She missed part of the lesson. _____

6. This week, Fiona enters the class on time. _____

B. Write one sentence with a verb in the present tense and one sentence with a verb in the past tense.

7. Present: _____

8. Past: _____

Great Grammar Practice, Grade 2 © 2015 by Scholastic Teaching Resources

Name _____ Date _____

Future Tense Verbs

Verbs can tell about action in the future.

Future verbs have *will* in front of them.

Future: It will rain tomorrow.
                        ↑

A. Circle the verb in each sentence. Write **present**, **past**, or **future** to tell about the verb tense.

1. The rain flooded our yard last night. _____

2. It covered all the tree trunks. _____

3. Now Dad looks at the yard in dismay. _____

4. He takes a picture of the damage. _____

5. The water will disappear soon. _____

6. Then we will clean up the yard. _____

B. Write two sentences that show action in the future.

7. _____

8. _____

Great Grammar Practice, Grade 2 © 2015 by Scholastic Teaching Resources

More About Verbs

Some past tense verbs do not end in the regular way.

PRESENT	PAST
sit/sits	sat
get/gets	got
run/runs	ran
hold/holds	held

PRESENT	PAST
hide/hides	hid
tell/tells	told
eat/eats	ate
wear/wears	wore

A. Circle the verb in each sentence. Write **present** or **past** to tell about the verb tense.

1. Uma sits at a table in a restaurant. _____

2. She wears her new dress. _____

3. A minute ago, she ate something spicy. _____

4. She told the waiter right away. _____

5. He ran for a glass of water. _____

6. He quickly got the water for Uma. _____

B. Write two sentences that show the past. Choose verbs from the charts above.

7. _____

8. _____

Name _____ Date _____

Using *Is/Are* and *Was/Were*

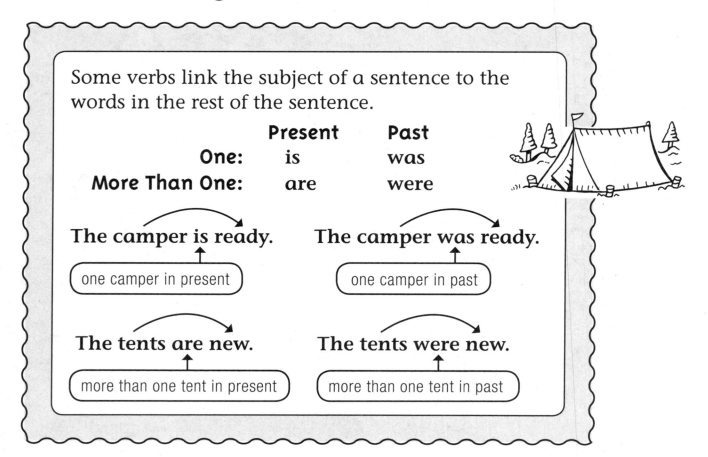

Some verbs link the subject of a sentence to the words in the rest of the sentence.

	Present	Past
One:	is	was
More Than One:	are	were

The camper is ready.

one camper in present

The camper was ready.

one camper in past

The tents are new.

more than one tent in present

The tents were new.

more than one tent in past

A. Write **is** or **are** in each sentence to show the present.

1. The tents _____ green.

2. The campers _____ here.

3. Tori's tent _____ there.

4. My tent _____ small.

5. Some campers _____ sleepy.

6. My sleeping bag _____ warm.

B. Underline the correct sentence to show the past.

7. a. Blake was awake.

b. Blake were awake.

8. a. The bugs was busy.

b. The bugs were busy.

9. a. Ron's flashlight was on.

b. Ron's flashlight were on.

Name _____ Date _____

Using *Has* and *Have*

Use the verb *has* with one person or thing.

Use the verb *have* with more than one person or thing.

Use *have* with the pronouns *I* and *you*.

We have a treehouse. Our treehouse has a ladder.

(more than one person)   (one treehouse)

I have fun in it. You have fun, too.

(pronoun *I*)   (pronoun *you*)

A. Write **has** or **have** in each sentence.

1. The treehouse _____ a door.   **2.** It _____ a window.

3. We _____ furniture there.   **4.** I _____ toys there.

5. You _____ lunch there.   **6.** Some birds _____ a nest in the tree.

B. Underline the correct sentence.

7. a. The tree has big branches.   **b.** The tree have big branches.

8. a. The branches has many leaves.   **b.** The branches have many leaves.

9. a. I has a rug in the treehouse.   **b.** I have a rug in the treehouse.

Great Grammar Practice, Grade 2 © 2015 by Scholastic Teaching Resources

What Is a Contraction?

A verb and the word *not* can combine to make a smaller word called a contraction.

The letter *o* is left out. An apostrophe ' takes the place of the missing letter.

Verb and *Not*:	is not	did not	was not
Contraction:	isn't	didn't	wasn't

A. Write the two words for each contraction.

1. don't _____   **2.** aren't _____

3. didn't _____   **4.** hasn't _____

5. haven't _____   **6.** weren't _____

B. Read the first sentence. In the second sentence, write the contraction for the underlined words.

7. Jody <u>is not</u> here. No, she _____ here.

8. She <u>was not</u> well yesterday. She _____ well at all.

9. She <u>did not</u> eat her lunch. She _____ play either.

10. She <u>could not</u> do her math. She _____ read her book.

    Great Grammar Practice, Grade 2 © 2015 by Scholastic Teaching Resources

Name _____ Date _____

Using Contractions

A verb and the word *not* can combine to make a smaller word called a contraction.

The letter *o* is left out. An apostrophe *'* takes the place of the missing letter.

Verb and *Not*: do not   **Contraction:** don't

Some contractions are not formed in the regular way.

Verb and *Not*: will not   cannot

Contraction: won't   can't

A. Write a contraction for each set of words.

1. should not _____   **2.** are not _____

3. will not _____   **4.** do not _____

5. were not _____   **6.** cannot _____

B. Read the first sentence. In the second sentence, write the contraction for the underlined words.

7. Scott <u>will not</u> go to the skating rink.

He _____ be there.

8. He <u>cannot</u> find his skates.

He _____ find them anywhere.

Great Grammar Practice, Grade 2 © 2015 by Scholastic Teaching Resources

Review: Verbs

A verb is an action word. It tells what someone or something is doing, will do, or has done.

WORD BANK

build	can't	was
didn't	like	isn't
will go	liked	likes
crawl	wants	is

Choose the best verb from the word bank to complete each sentence.

1. Next week, Mateo's family _____ camping.

2. Alicia _____ hiking the best.

3. Dad and Mom _____ bird-watching.

4. Mom and Alicia always _____ the campfire.

5. Last summer, Dad _____ our only cook.

6. We _____ his cooking a lot.

7. He _____ burn any of the food!

8. This time, Mateo _____ to help him.

9. After dinner, we all _____ into our tents.

10. The family _____ wait!

   Great Grammar Practice, Grade 2 © 2015 by Scholastic Teaching Resources

Name _____ Date _____

What Is an Adjective?

An adjective is a word that describes a noun.

An adjective can tell size, shape, and color.

Pippa sits in a big, red chair with square pillows.

(size of chair) (color of chair) (shape of pillows)

A. Circle the adjective in each sentence.

1. A tall lamp stands near the chair.

2. Pippa wears a green top.

3. She reads a book about a small lamb.

4. The chair has round spots on it.

B. Look at the picture. Then choose the best adjective from the word bank to complete each sentence. Use each word only once.

WORD BANK

wide

blue

square

long

5. Pippa has _____ hair.

6. She sits on a _____ cushion.

7. She has on her _____ jeans.

8. Pippa can put up her feet in the _____ chair.

More Adjectives

An adjective is a word that describes a noun.

An adjective can tell how many.

An adjective can describe the senses: sight, touch, sound, taste, and smell.

HOW MANY	SIGHT	TOUCH	SOUND	TASTE	SMELL
two	large	sticky	quiet	sweet	stinky
many	dark	silky	noisy	dry	rotten
few	empty	itchy	rustling	sour	sharp

A. Read each sentence. Write the word that suggests one of the senses.

1. The itchy straw made Kiri sneeze. _____

2. The crackers were stale. _____

3. Tony could smell the fresh air at the beach. _____

4. A booming sound woke up the baby. _____

5. A yellow pear grew on the tree. _____

B. Circle the adjective in each sentence.

6. Nils got five stars on his paper.

7. Donna ate two apples.

8. There were many balloons in the air.

Name _____ Date _____

Adjectives and Nouns

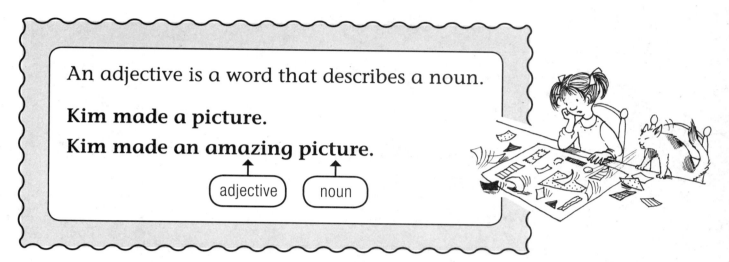

An adjective is a word that describes a noun.

Kim made a picture.

Kim made an amazing picture.

adjective   noun

A. Reach each sentence. Circle the adjective and underline the noun it describes.

1. Kim cut small pieces of paper.

2. Kim's funny cat watched.

3. Kim made many shapes.

4. She tried different designs.

5. A colorful design filled the page.

6. Then the naughty cat walked on it!

B. Write two adjectives to describe each noun.

7. top _____

_____

9. sled _____

_____

8. wagon _____

_____

10. drum _____

_____

Great Grammar Practice, Grade 2 © 2015 by Scholastic Teaching Resources

Name _____   Date _____

What Is an Adverb?

An adverb is a word that describes a verb.

An adverb tells when, where, or how an action happens.

When: We visited the castle <u>today</u>.

Where: We rode <u>there</u>.

How: We pedaled <u>fast</u>.

A. The verb in each sentence is underlined. Circle the adverb that describes the verb.

1. We <u>wait</u> at the castle now.

2. The keeper <u>will come</u> soon.

3. He <u>arrives</u> here on time.

4. We <u>greet</u> him happily.

5. He <u>opens</u> the gate quickly.

6. We <u>follow</u> him excitedly.

B. Underline the verb in each sentence. Then choose the best adverb from the word bank to complete each sentence.

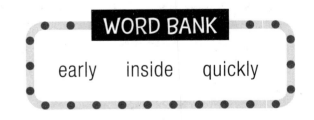

WORD BANK

early   inside   quickly

7. A dragon lives _____!

8. The dragon awakes from his nap _____.

9. We leave the castle _____!

 Great Grammar Practice, Grade 2 © 2015 by Scholastic Teaching Resources

More Adverbs

> An adverb is a word that describes a verb.
>
> An adverb tells when, where, or how an action happens.
>
> | WHEN | WHERE | HOW |
> |------|-------|-----|
> | today | there | swiftly |
> | tomorrow | everywhere | strongly |
> | earlier | anywhere | carefully |

A. Read each sentence. Write a word that suggests when, where, or how.

1. We visited the lake _____.

2. It took a long time to get _____.

3. We drove _____.

4. The wind was blowing _____.

5. Our boat sailed _____.

6. We want to return _____.

B. Read the words below. Cross out the word in each set that is not an adverb.

7. never
seven
slowly
yesterday

8. later
easily
sunny
perfectly

9. outside
gladly
upstairs
purple

Adverbs and Verbs

An adverb is a word that describes a verb.

It rained. It rained today.

verb   adverb

A. Read each sentence. Underline the verb. Circle the adverb that describes the verb.

1. The rain fell heavily.

2. Mrs. Greene walked rapidly.

3. She held the umbrella tightly.

B. Read the verbs on the left and the adverbs on the right. Draw a line to connect each verb to an adverb that is a good partner.

4. tip-toe   **a.** loudly

5. laugh   **b.** kindly

6. answer   **c.** sadly

7. cry   **d.** softly

8. help   **e.** politely

Review: Adjectives and Adverbs

An adjective describes a noun. An adverb describes a verb.

Six children stand in line. The students stand silently.

A. Circle the noun in each sentence. Write an adjective from the word bank to describe it.

1. A _____ bell rang.

2. The _____ school listened.

3. The _____ teacher led the class.

4. It was a _____ drill.

B. Circle the verb in each sentence. Write an adverb from the word bank to describe it.

5. The drills happen _____.

6. Students walk _____.

7. They listen _____ to the teacher.

8. Safety matters _____.

WORD BANK	
ADJECTIVES	**ADVERBS**
calm	greatly
clanging	outside
practice	carefully
whole	often

Name _____   Date _____

Where Words

A preposition is a word that can help tell where something is.

The kite is over the ground.

where the kite is

PREPOSITIONS				
on	under	over	beside	to
near	above	around	into	by
in	along	onto	between	at

A. Match the words on the left to the phrase on the right that tells where in the picture each thing is.

1. bird

2. kite

3. rabbits

4. bee

a. behind the girl

b. above the bird

c. on the branch

d. in the air

B. Circle the preposition in each sentence.

5. The girl holds onto the string.

6. Flowers grow near the tree.

7. The girl has a bow on her head.

8. The rabbits run along the ground.

Name _____ Date _____

Building Sentences With Prepositions

A preposition is a word that can help tell where something is or when something happens. You can build sentences by adding phrases beginning with a preposition.

Theo liked eggs.

Theo liked eggs <u>in the morning</u>.

when Theo liked eggs

PREPOSITIONAL PHRASES
for school
in a basket
on the stove
under the hens
at the table
to the henhouse
into a pan
at dawn

Choose the best phrase from the list to build each sentence.

1. Each morning Theo awoke _____.

2. He walked _____.

3. He found eggs _____.

4. Theo carried the eggs _____.

5. His Mom put them _____.

6. She cooked them _____.

7. Theo sat _____.

8. Then he was ready _____.

Great Grammar Practice, Grade 2 © 2015 by Scholastic Teaching Resources

Name _____ Date _____

Review: Prepositions

A preposition is a word that can help tell where something is or when something happens.

WORD BANK

around	by
in	into
near	on
over	to
under	with

Choose the best preposition from the word bank to complete each sentence. Use each word only once.

1. _____ the afternoon, I took a walk.

2. I saw a very special dog _____ a flower patch.

3. He was dressed nicely and wore a hat _____ his head.

4. A crowd formed _____ the dog.

5. The people watched him juggle four balls _____ his head.

6. The balls flew _____ the air.

7. He caught each one _____ his paws.

8. An amazed man pointed _____ the dog.

9. The grass was soft _____ everyone's feet.

10. There was a butterfly _____ the action.

 Great Grammar Practice, Grade 2 © 2015 by Scholastic Teaching Resources

Name _____ Date _____

Using Capital Letters

Sentences begin with capital letters.

Proper nouns begin also with capital letters.

We played baseball with Kira's bat.

↑   ↑

capital letter   capital letter

Rewrite each sentence correctly. Use capital letters where they are needed.

1. tomorrow is saturday and we have a big game.

_____

2. our team is called the bayview bears.

_____

3. are we playing against the central tigers?

_____

4. usually, i play in left field.

_____

5. i hope that jamie hits the ball.

_____

Great Grammar Practice, Grade 2 © 2015 by Scholastic Teaching Resources

Name _____ Date _____

Using Commas

Commas separate words in a series.

Mom had a suitcase, purse, and camera.

commas separate words in series

Complete each sentence with the person's list. Use commas to separate the words in a series.

JED'S LIST
backpack
book
game

1. Jed took a _____

_____ .

HONEY'S LIST
bear
pillow
snack

2. Honey brought a _____

_____ .

DAD'S LIST
magazine
briefcase
computer

3. Dad carried a _____

_____ .

GRANDMA'S LIST
skirt
sweater
blouse
scarf

4. In Grandma's bag she had an extra _____

_____ .

Name _____   Date _____

Writing Dates

The name of each month is a proper noun.

It begins with a capital letter.

A comma comes between the day and the year in a date.

December 31, 2015

month | day followed by comma | year

Write each date correctly.

1. october 15 2006   _____

2. june 21 1960   _____

3. february 2 2015   _____

4. september 30 1998   _____

5. july 4 1776   _____

6. your birthday   _____

7. today's date   _____

8. yesterday's date   _____

Great Grammar Practice, Grade 2 © 2015 by Scholastic Teaching Resources

Name _____ Date _____

Writing a Letter

A comma comes between the day and year in a date.

A comma follows the greeting and closing in a letter.

The greeting and first word of the closing begin with a capital letter.

July 2, 2015 ← comma between day and year

Dear Uncle Alex, ← begins with capital letter; comma after greeting

Thank you for the book you sent for my birthday. I have wanted to read it for a long time. Now I can!

Your niece, ← first word begins with capital letter; comma after closing

Sue

Rewrite the letter correctly. Use capital letters and commas where they are needed.

may 5 2015

dear kurt

we are looking forward to your visit this summer. your cousin luke can't wait! bring your swimsuit. we will go to the beach every day.

lots of love

aunt rosa

_____

_____

_____

_____

_____

_____

_____

Name _____ Date _____

Using Apostrophes

An apostrophe with an *s* can make a noun possessive. It can also help turn a verb phrase into a contraction.

Amir's room

apostrophe; possessive

is not → isn't

apostrophe; contraction

A. Complete each sentence below. Use a noun from the word bank and make it possessive.

1. The _____ whiskers are long.

2. My _____ room is neat.

3. The _____ nest was in the tree.

4. Did you taste _____ macaroni?

WORD BANK

Mom
bird
brother
cat

B. Complete each sentence below. Use a verb phrase from the word bank and turn it into a contraction.

5. They _____ at home now.

6. Felix _____ on time.

7. It's hot, so _____ touch it.

8. Jenna _____ go to the party.

WORD BANK

are not
did not
was not
do not

Name _____ Date _____

Review: Capitalization and Punctuation

Using capitals and correct punctuation makes a sentence easier to read. Remember to use capitals at the beginning of sentences and proper nouns.

End punctuation shows what kind of sentence it is.

Commas separate words in a series.

Write each sentence correctly. Use capitals where they are needed and end punctuation. Use commas to separate words in a series.

1. the sand at the beach is white gritty and warm

_____

2. why can't you visit us on thanksgiving

_____

3. the children in this group are ryan gabrielle and justin

_____

4. where are the slide swings and treehouse

_____

5. watch out

_____

Name _____ Date _____

Vowel Sounds

Vowel sounds can be spelled in different ways.

SOUND	SPELLINGS			EXAMPLES		
Long a	ai	ay		rain	play	
Long e	ee	ea	e	keep	meat	me
Long i	i	y	igh	find	cry	night
Long o	o	oa	ow	most	boat	grow
/ü/ as in *soon*	oo	ew		cool	new	

Write a long vowel or /ü/ word for each picture.

1.  _____

2. _____

3. _____

4. _____

5. _____

6. _____

7.  _____

8.  _____

Great Grammar Practice, Grade 2 © 2015 by Scholastic Teaching Resources

Name _____ Date _____

Blending Sounds

Some words begin with two consonants that blend together as one sound.

CONSONANT + L	CONSONANT + R
bl, cl, fl, gl, pl, sl	br, cr, dr, fr, gr, pr, tr, wr
blue, clay, flag, glee, plum, sled	break, crew, draw, from, grow, pretty, tree, wrist

CONSONANT + W	CONSONANT + M	CONSONANT + T
sw, tw	sm	st
swing, twin	smell	star

Circle the blended sounds that begin each word.

1. plan

2. cream

3. flock

4. smoke

5. blob

6. price

7. grain

8. stall

9. drum

10. slip

11. brown

12. sweet

Name _____ Date _____

Double Letters

Some sounds are spelled with double consonants that have one sound.

DOUBLE CONSONANTS	EXAMPLES
ll	tell, sill, call
ss	mess, loss, fuss
ff	off, cuff, cliff
bb	dribble, bubble
pp	happy, drippy

A. Add the letters to form words that are spelled with double consonants. Choose from the list of double consonants above.

1. cla_____

2. du_____

3. bu_____le

4. pe_____er

5. o_____er

6. se_____

B. Write a word spelled with double consonants to name each picture.

7.  _____

8. _____

9. _____

10. _____

Great Grammar Practice, Grade 2 © 2015 by Scholastic Teaching Resources

Name _____ Date _____

Word Families

Some words can be grouped into families because they have the same spelling base.

-IGHT	-ILL	-OCK
flight	grill	dock
knight	thrill	lock
sight	will	knock

Write the beginning sound and the base sound to make a noun. Then write the plural for each noun. The first one is done for you.

1. dr + ill = <u>drill</u>   <u>drills</u>

2. s + ock = _____ _____

3. h + ill = _____ _____

4. l + ight = _____ _____

5. r + ock = _____ _____

6. ch + ill = _____ _____

7. n + ight = _____ _____

8. cl + ock = _____ _____

9. s + ight = _____ _____

Great Grammar Practice, Grade 2 © 2015 by Scholastic Teaching Resources

Name _____ Date _____

What Is a Prefix?

A prefix is a group of letters at the beginning of a word that changes the word's meaning.

WORD	PREFIX AND MEANING	NEW WORD
write	*re-* meaning "again"	rewrite

Complete each sentence with a word that has the prefix **re-**. Use the word bank to help you.

WORD BANK

reheat   relearn
relock   remake
reread   resend
reuse   rewatch

1. When you read a story again,

you _____ it.

2. If you use something more than once, you _____ it.

3. When you _____ your bed, you make it again.

4. If you learn something again, you _____ it.

5. Lily liked that movie, so she will _____ it.

6. The food is cold, so we will _____ it.

7. When you close the door, remember to _____ it.

8. I didn't get your e-mail. Can you _____ it?

Name _____ Date _____

What Is a Suffix?

A suffix is a group of letters at the end of a word that changes the word's meaning. It can also change the word from one part of speech to another.

WORD	PART OF SPEECH	SUFFIX AND MEANING	NEW WORD	PART OF SPEECH
paint	verb	-er meaning "a person who"	painter	noun

Complete each sentence with a word that has the suffix **-er**.
Use the word bank to help you.

WORD BANK

baker	builder
climber	farmer
writer	listener
singer	speaker

1. Someone who farms is

a _____ .

2. If you listen well, you are a good _____ .

3. Someone who bakes foods is a _____ .

4. A _____ is a person who sings songs.

5. If you climb a mountain, you are a _____ .

6. A _____ is a person who writes.

7. If your job is to build things, you are a _____ .

8. A _____ is a person who is speaking.

Review: Spelling

When you read a word, think about the sounds of its letters. Vowel sounds can be spelled in different ways.

Some words begin or end with consonants that blend together as one sound.

Some letters might be silent.

WORD BANK

cool	find	me
new	night	play

A. Write a long vowel or /ü/ word that is the opposite of each word below. Use the word bank to help you.

1. lose _____   **2.** old _____   **3.** day _____

4. you _____   **5.** rest _____   **6.** warm _____

B. Write two words that begin with the blend in each word below. Use a dictionary for help.

7. club

_____

_____

8. glum

_____

_____

9. bridge

_____

_____

10. twig

_____

_____

11. swim

_____

_____

12. slide

_____

_____

Activity 1: A. 1. sentence 2. sentence 3. sentence 4. not a sentence 5. not a sentence 6. sentence B. 7.–8. Check that students write complete sentences.

Activity 2: 1. a 2. b 3. a 4. b B. 5. b 6. a

Activity 3: Answers will vary. Possible: 1. man 2. girl 3. boy 4. Kevin 5. cat 6. dish 7. woman or mother 8. dog

Activity 4: 1. cools 2. sweeps 3. bounces 4. rings 5. waves 6. measures 7. ticks 8. rocks

Activity 5: 1. d 2. f 3. c 4. a 5. b 6. e 7. h 8. g

Activity 6: A. 1. statement 2. statement 3. question 4. question 5. statement 6. question B. 7. Check that students complete the statement. 8. Check that students complete the question.

Activity 7: 1. How many runners are on a team? 2. How far will they run? 3. The race is on the track. 4. Is everyone ready?

Activity 8: A. 1. command 2. command 3. statement 4. statement B. 5. exclamation 6. command 7. command 8. exclamation

Activity 9: 1. Pass the ball. 2. Wow! 3. Guard that player. 4. Nice play! 5. Make that shot. 6. Great game!

Activity 10: A. 1.–4. Check that students label both ideas and add *and* to each sentence. B. 5.–6. Answers will vary.

Activity 11: A. 1.–4. Check that students label both ideas and add *because* to each sentence. B. 5.–6. Answers will vary.

Activity 12: A. 1. period; statement 2. question mark; question 3. period; command 4. question mark; question 5. exclamation point; exclamation 6. period; statement B. 7. We ate our lunch at the park.

Activity 13: A. 1. policeman 2. city 3. saddle B. 4. horse 5. tail 6. street 7. window 8. cloud

Activity 14: A. 1. Becca Hardy; Rocky Mountains 2. Salt Lake City; San Francisco 3. Mia Grasso; Columbus Day B. 4. Thanksgiving 5. April Fool's Day 6. Independence Day or Fourth of July 7. Valentine's Day C. 8. Check that students write the city name correctly.

Activity 15: A. 1. nuts 2. bags; beans 3. carrots 4. hotdogs; rolls B. 5. grapes 6. cheese 7. cakes 8. pies

Activity 16: 1. The geese flew over the houses. 2. The children chased after the balls. 3. The mice ran when the women screamed. 4. The men hitched the oxen to a cart. 5. The socks covered Ella's feet.

Activity 17: A. 1. flock 2. pride 3. school 4. gaggle B. 5. ants 6. apes 7. bees 8. dogs

Activity 18: A. 1. Jamie's 2. brother's 3. friend's 4. Dad's B. 5. Mom's 6. Ada's

Activity 19: A. 1. swing; it 2. Carson; He 3. kids; They 4. Polly; She B. 5. He 6. She 7. It 8. They

Activity 20: 1. I; Jada 2. you; Jada 3. you; Owen 4. me; Owen 5. I; Jada 6. Me; Jada 7. We; Owen and Jada 8. you; Owen

Activity 21: 1. herself 2. himself 3. themselves 4. itself 5. myself 6. yourself 7. ourselves

Activity 22: 1. He; Wyatt 2. She; Mother 3. They; pigs 4. it; game 5. They; pigs and Wyatt 5. He; Wyatt

Activity 23: A. 1. needed 2. drooped 3. gave 4. got 5. took B. 6. liked 7. put 8. thanked

Activity 24: 1. fear 2. likes 3. builds 4. makes 5. destroys 6. fool 7. designs

Activity 25: A. 1. waits; present 2. directs; present 3. fill; present 4. arrived; past 5. missed; past 6. enters; present B. 7.–8. Answers will vary.

Activity 26: A. 1. flooded; past 2. covered; past 3. looks; present 4. takes; present 5. will disappear; future 6. will clean; future B. 7.–8. Answers will vary.

Activity 27: A. 1. sits; present 2. wears; present 3. ate; past 4. told; past 5. ran; past 6. got; past B. 7.–8. Answers will vary.

Activity 28: A. 1. are 2. are 3. is 4. is 5. are 6. is B. 7. a 8. b 9. a

Activity 29: A. 1. has 2. has 3. have 4. have 5. have 6. have B. 7. a 8. b 9. b

Activity 30: A. 1. do not 2. are not 3. did not 4. has not 5. have not 6. were not B. 7. isn't 8. wasn't 9. didn't 10. couldn't

Activity 31: A. 1. shouldn't 2. aren't 3. won't 4. don't 5. weren't 6. can't B. 7. won't 8. can't

Activity 32: 1. will go 2. likes 3. like 4. build 5. was 6. liked 7. didn't 8. wants 9. crawl 10. can't

Activity 33: A. 1. tall 2. green 3. small 4. round 5. long 6. square 7. blue 8. wide

Activity 34: A. 1. itchy 2. stale 3. fresh 4. booming 5. yellow B. 6. five 7. two 8. many

Activity 35: A. 1. small; <u>pieces</u> 2. funny; <u>cat</u> 3. many; <u>shapes</u> 4. different; <u>designs</u> 5. colorful; <u>design</u> 6. naughty; <u>cat</u> B. 7.–10. Check that students describe the items pictured.

Activity 36: A. 1. now 2. soon 3. here 4. happily 5. quickly 6. excitedly B. 7. <u>lives</u>; inside 8. <u>awakes</u>; early 9. <u>leave</u>; quickly

Activity 37: A. Answers will vary. Possible: 1. today 2. there 3. carefully 4. strongly 5. swiftly 6. tomorrow B. 7. seven 8. sunny 9. purple

Activity 38: A. 1. <u>fell</u>; heavily 2. <u>walked</u>; rapidly 3. <u>held</u>; tightly B. 4. d 5. a 6. e 7. c 8. b

Activity 39: A. 1. clanging; bell 2. whole; school 3. calm; teacher 4. practice; drills B. 5. happen; often 6. walk; outside 7. listen; carefully 8. matters; greatly

Activity 40: A. 1. c 2. d 3. a 4. b B. 5. onto 6. near 7. on 8. along

Activity 41: 1. at dawn 2. to the henhouse 3. under the hens 4. in a basket 5. into a pan 6. on the stove 7. at the table 8. for school

Activity 42: 1. In 2. by 3. on 4. around 5. over 6. into 7. with 8. to 9. under 10. near

Activity 43: When rewriting the sentences, students should capitalize the following words: 1. Tomorrow; Saturday 2. Our; Bayview Bears 3. Are; Central Tigers 4. Usually; I 5. I; Jamie

Activity 44: 1. Jed took a backpack, book, and game. 2. Honey brought a bear, pillow, and snack. 3. Dad carried a magazine, briefcase, and computer. 4. In Grandma's bag she had an extra skirt, sweater, blouse, and scarf.

Activity 45: 1. October 15, 2006 2. June 21, 1960 3. February 2, 2015 4. September 30, 1998 5. July 4, 1776 6.–8. Check that students write each date correctly.

Activity 46:

May 5, 2015

Dear Kurt,

We are looking forward to your visit this summer. Your cousin Luke can't wait! Bring your swimsuit. We will go to the beach every day.

Lots of love,

Aunt Rosa

Activity 47: A. 1. cat's 2. brother's 3. bird's 4. Mom's B. 5. aren't 6. wasn't 7. don't 8. didn't

Activity 48: 1. The sand at the beach is white, gritty, and warm. 2. Why can't you visit us on Thanksgiving? 3. The children in this group are Ryan, Gabrielle, and Justin. 4. Where are the slide, swings, and treehouse? 5. Watch out!

Activity 49: 1. train 2. coat 3. tray 4. three 5. bow 6. beans 7. moon 8. cry

Activity 50: 1. pl 2. cr 3. fl 4. sm 5. bl 6. pr 7. gr 8. st 9. dr 10. sl 11. br 12. sw

Activity 51: A. 1. class 2. dull 3. bubble 4. pepper 5. offer 6. sell B. 7. bell 8. puppy 9. rabbit or bunny 10. ball

Activity 52: 1. drill; drills 2. sock; socks 3. hill; hills 4. light; lights 5. rock; rocks 6. chill; chills 7. night; nights 8. clock; clocks 9. sight; sights

Activity 53: 1. reread 2. reuse 3. remake 4. relearn 5. rewatch 6. reheat 7. relock 8. resend

Activity 54: 1. farmer 2. listener 3. baker 4. singer 5. climber 6. writer 7. builder 8. speaker

Activity 55: A. 1. find 2. new 3. night 4. me 5. play 6. cool B. Answers will vary. Possible: 7. clam; climb 8. glue; glide 9. bring; bride 10. twin; twice 11. swan; swipe 12. slope; slam